ABDO
Publishing Company

Biking

MOVE YOUR BODY

A Kid's Guide to Fitness

A Buddy Book by **Sarah Tieck**

VISIT US AT
www.abdopublishing.com

Published by ABDO Publishing Company, PO Box 398166, Minneapolis, MN 55439.

Printed in the United States of America, North Mankato, Minnesota.
092012
012013

 PRINTED ON RECYCLED PAPER

Coordinating Series Editor: Rochelle Baltzer
Contributing Editors: Stephanie Hedlund, Marcia Zappa
Graphic Design: Jenny Christensen
Cover Photograph: *iStockphoto*: ©iStockphoto.com/carlofranco.
Interior Photographs/Illustrations: *Eighth Street Studio* (p. 26); *Glow Images*: Superstock (p. 11); *iStockphoto*: ©iStockphoto.com/Andyworks (p. 9), ©iStockphoto.com/ bowdenimages (p. 5), ©iStockphoto.com/dstephens (p. 7), ©iStockphoto.com/Mari (p. 17), ©iStockphoto.com/mo64 (p. 23), ©iStockphoto.com/stevecoleimages (p. 25), ©iStockphoto.com/Syldavia (p. 25); *Shutterstock*: a9photo (p. 27), AVAVA (p. 26), Vaidas Bucys (p. 15), fotum (p. 19), Warren Goldswain (p. 30), Geir Olav Lyngfjell (p. 9), Aleksandr Markin (p. 13), Dmitry Naumov (p. 15), PHB.cz (Richard Semik) (p. 30), Dmitriy Shironosov (p. 21), spotmatik (p. 29), Dmitry Yashkin (p. 9), YorkBerlin (p. 13).

Library of Congress Cataloging-in-Publication Data

Tieck, Sarah, 1976-
  Biking / Sarah Tieck.
     p. cm. -- (Move your body: a kid's guide to fitness)
  ISBN 978-1-61783-560-5
1. Cycling--Juvenile literature. I. Title.
GV1043.5.T54 2013
  796.6--dc23
                                    2012023908

Table of Contents

Healthy Living

Your body is amazing! A healthy body helps you feel good and live well. In order to be healthy, you must take care of yourself. One way to do this is to move your body.

Regular movement gives you **energy** and makes you stronger. Many kinds of exercise can help you do this. One fun type of exercise is biking! Let's learn more about biking.

Children should get 60 minutes of movement every day. Biking is one way to do this.

Most people bike outdoors. But, some people bike indoors. They use stationary bikes at a gym or at home.

WORD OF MOUTH

Biking 101

Bikers move their bodies on bikes. They turn the pedals with their feet and legs. They use their hands and arms to change direction. And, they use their **abdominal** and back **muscles** to balance. This helps hold the bike upright.

Rides can be long or short. They can also be easy or hard. This depends on where you go and how hard you pedal.

Steep hills and unpaved paths can make a bike ride harder.

Many people learn to ride a bike with training wheels. This helps them balance. When they are ready, these extra wheels are removed. Then, they can practice on two wheels.

After learning basic riding skills, you can try different types of biking. You could mountain bike on paths in the wild. You could race on roads or a track. You could even do **stunts**!

The first bikes were invented more than 150 years ago. Today, there are many different types of bikes.

WORD OF MOUTH

Different kinds of bikes are used for road racing (*above*), mountain biking (*right*), and doing stunts (*below*).

Let's Get Physical

People exercise to stay fit. Regular exercise makes it easier for you to bend and move. It helps you stay at a healthy body weight. And, it helps prevent health problems later in life.

Biking is a type of **aerobic** exercise. It makes your **lungs** and heart work hard to get your body more **oxygen**. The more often you bike, the easier it will be to breathe and move.

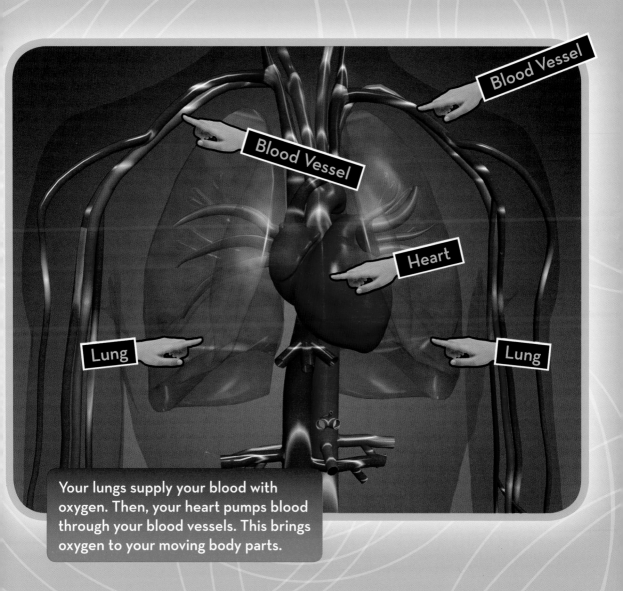

Blood Vessel

Blood Vessel

Heart

Lung

Lung

Your lungs supply your blood with oxygen. Then, your heart pumps blood through your blood vessels. This brings oxygen to your moving body parts.

Biking also builds your **muscles**. When you pedal a bike, you work your leg muscles. Over time, these muscles will get stronger. This will help you pedal more easily.

Pedaling uses the muscles on the front and back of your leg.

Gluteus

Quadriceps

Hamstring Muscles

Calf Muscle

Gearing Up

It is important to choose the right size bike for you. When sitting, the balls of your feet should touch the ground.

Next, make sure you have a helmet that fits properly. It should be worn level and not tipped back. You can move the straps so it is snug but comfortable.

Wear bright-colored clothes and put reflectors on your bike. This will help others see you.

Play It Safe

Every year, kids are hurt in biking accidents. Some even have to stay in the hospital. So, it is important to be careful.

The most serious harm when biking is to a person's head. So, you should always wear a helmet when you bike. This **protects** your head and brain if you fall or are hit while riding.

When you put on your helmet, fasten the straps. Make sure the helmet is tight enough to stay in place.

The US government has standards for safe helmets. These helmets have a special label.

WORD OF MOUTH

Don't wear headphones while you bike. This makes it hard to hear what is going on around you.

WORD OF MOUTH

When you bike, wear clothes that are comfortable. Be sure pants are fitted enough that they won't get caught in your bike chain.

Choose shoes that won't slip on the pedals. Flip-flops, dress shoes, or bare feet make it hard to pedal safely.

Sneakers are good shoes for biking.

Ready? Set? Go!

Warming up, cooling down, and stretching are important parts of exercise. Warm up with light movements before biking. This prepares your **muscles** to work hard.

Cool down after riding with slow, easy movements to help prevent sore muscles. Also take time to stretch. Over time, this makes it easier for your body to move.

To warm up for biking, just ride slowly. You could also walk or do jumping jacks.

Look and Learn

When you ride your bike, be aware of your surroundings. On the road, watch for cars and trucks and obey traffic laws. On the sidewalk, watch for walkers and runners. And, look for cars and trucks at driveways and crossings.

If you are on a trail, there are different things to watch for. There may be tree branches or uneven surfaces to ride around.

WORD OF MOUTH

Kids younger than ten should avoid riding on the road. They should stick to sidewalks and bike paths.

Left Turn

Use hand signals before you turn or stop. These tell drivers and other bikers what you are going to do.

Right Turn

Stop

Take Care

It is important that your bike is in good condition. Before you ride, ask an adult to check the tires for air. Ask him or her to check the brakes and oil the chain. Make sure the seat, handlebars, and wheels are secure.

Ask an adult to help you tighten the bolts and screws on your bike. This prevents parts from coming loose while you ride.

People use bike pumps to add air to tires.

WORD OF MOUTH

A special tool can tell you how much air each tire has. You can also just press on the tire. If it feels soft, it might need more air.

Brain Food

How do you know if you are biking hard enough to get a workout?

Some people just pay attention to how their bodies feel. Others measure their heart rate. This is the number of times your heart beats per minute.

A tool called a heart rate monitor measures this. You can also find it on your own. Touch the inside of your wrist or the side of your neck. Then, count the pulses you feel in one minute.

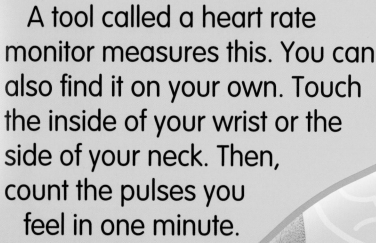

I'm scared I might crash when riding my bike! What can I do?

When you are riding, you might feel unsteady. Just keep practicing and training to become stronger. While you are doing this, wear elbow and knee pads to feel safer. Also, stay off of roads until you feel sure of yourself.

What is the best food to eat for biking?

Your body needs foods from each food group. But, foods in the **protein** group are especially helpful for biking. These help your body build and heal **muscles**. Protein-rich foods include meats, seafood, beans, eggs, and nuts. The best choices are lean, or low in fat.

Choose to Move

Remember that biking makes your body stronger. Ride as often as you can! Fitness is an important part of a healthy life. Each positive choice you make will help you stay healthy.

Biking is a fun family activity!

GROW STRONG

- ✔ Set a **goal** to improve your biking. Most bikers use distance or time to measure their progress.

- ✔ Exercises such as squats, lunges, and sit-ups can help improve your biking. That's because they strengthen your **muscles**!

DRINK UP

- ✔ Water plays an important part in helping your body build muscle.

- ✔ When you sweat, your body loses water. So, drink lots of water before, during, and after biking.

STAY SAFE

- ✔ After a fall off your bike, replace your helmet for safety. Some parts of it may be broken from the fall.

- ✔ Wear sunscreen to **protect** your skin if you ride outdoors. If you sweat a lot, choose a water-resistant kind.

Important Words

abdominal relating to the part of the body between the chest and the hips.

aerobic (ehr-OH-bihk) relating to exercise that increases oxygen in the body and makes the heart better able to use oxygen.

energy (EH-nuhr-jee) the power or ability to do things.

goal something that a person works to reach or complete.

lungs body parts that help the body breathe.

muscle (MUH-suhl) body tissue, or layers of cells, that helps move the body.

oxygen (AHK-sih-juhn) a colorless gas that humans and animals need to breathe.

protect (pruh-TEHKT) to guard against harm or danger.

protein (PROH-teen) an important part of the diet of all animals.

stunt an action requiring great skill or daring.

Web Sites

To learn more about biking, visit ABDO Publishing Company online. Web sites about biking are featured on our Book Links page. These links are routinely monitored and updated to provide the most current information available.

www.abdopublishing.com

Index